JONATHAN SELIGER

FLOOR MODEL

IAN BERRY

THE TANG TEACHING MUSEUM AND ART GALLERY

SKIDMORE COLLEGE

FLOOR MODEL: A Dialogue with JONATHAN SELIGER by Ian Berry

Immersed in the desires of poetry and the vocabulary of contemporary art, Jonathan Seliger began making paintings eleven years ago
in New York City. His canvases combine techniques of painting,
printmaking, and sculpture and are stretched, folded and glued to
form recognizable everyday objects. The familiar, in the form of
envelopes, pillows and shopping bags, to name just a few, is trans-
formed through the artist's precise attention to detail and surreal
alterations of scale and color into carefully wrought works that
are equal parts abstract and revealing. Psychology, autobiography
and art history inhabit these witty and seductive objects. While
deciphering Seliger's puzzles, curiosity gives way to empathy.
Along the way these one-of-a-kind consumer trophies take hold
like the protective and slightly embarrassed glee that comes
uncontrollably with a lucky find.

IB Let's begin with your decision to make art. What prompted
you to begin painting after trying your hand at writing?

JS I grew up with a picture of myself as a writer. I majored in
English and Comparative Literature and I studied creative writing
with the poet John Ashbery. The collage, aleatory, non-linear but
very urban idiom that he devised was very influential — cultural
fragmentation, but not of the sheet-chewing variety, more cut and
paste experience. Following Ashbery's lead, and other poets of the
New York School, I became involved with art as an art critic and
independent curator, gallery director, and an editor at the Journal
of Contemporary Art. I then decided to put writing aside and
become an artist. Honestly, writing had dried up for me, and I
had always been attracted to the pleasures of painting. At first
I had no idea what I was going to do, I just started.

(title page)
Idealized Self-Portrait, 2000
Oil, alkyd, acrylic, modeling
paste and varnish on canvas;
lacquer and wax on bronze
84 x 16.25 x 5.5"
Collection of Michael & Sirje
Gold, Los Angeles

(facing page)
Little Colossus, 1997–98
Oil, alkyd, acrylic and soluvar
on polyester resin and fiber-
glass; latex on wood
Overall dimensions
12.75 x 18 x 10"
Collection of the artist

5

One Up, One Down, 1994
(front and back view)
Oil, alkyd, acrylic, modeling
paste, powdered graphite and
wire on cotton; acrylic, oil,
alkyd and watercolor on board
2 parts, 3.25 x 2.5 x .75"
and 2 x 2.5 x .75"
Marc & Livia Straus Family
Collection

IB You began making small objects like matchbooks and envelopes, what attracted you to this scale?

JS I started working small for a variety of reasons. First off there were technical obstacles to overcome. But moreover as a writer I was used to the experience of holding a book and looking at a printed page. The black and white nature of text on a page, the graphic quality of that, was very familiar to me. From the start, however, I was interested in a form that was "aware of its objectness," a form that was an amalgam of a painting and a sculpture.

IB Why build out in three dimensions instead of representing volumes with perspective?

JS After a few years of experimenting with different approaches I realized I was interested in representing objects but I became disinterested in painting the space around them. I took as a visual cue and point of departure what Jasper Johns posits as an equivalence between the support and the image — first in the flag paintings and later more structurally in the crosshatch paintings. In simple terms, Johns presents a painting of a flag and each of the sections of the flag has its own stretcher and canvas to hold that particular image/area. You have a panel for the stars, a panel for the stripes contiguous with the stars, and you have a panel for the stripes below. The image fills out the entire support. With all that locked into place he was free to make all these decisions with the brushwork that perhaps conflicted with or even cancelled the image. Likewise the crosshatch series are painted in primary, secondary and tertiary colors with clusters of five strokes going in alternate directions. His method was programmatic and intuitive. It's said that the paintings imply a three dimensional space, that if you took the painting off the stretcher and folded it in on itself,

top to bottom and side to side, there would be a continuous image. This may be my own creative misreading to grant myself license, but as a model it was useful to jog me over a hump. The idea that a flat structure would first fill out a plane and then move into space and support itself excited me.

IB Your choice of everyday subject matter is similar to the pop artists as well, although your choices feel more personal. Do the works function as personal metaphors?

JS Their worldliness is important. I like the specificity. Also their use value or uselessness had poetic resonance for me—a sense of fragility and mortality. As a writer I was interested in the secular poems of John Donne, like "The Good Morrow," "The Sun Rising," or "The Ecstasy." The set up of all these poems is the same: he's in bed with a lover and he doesn't want to get out of bed in the morning and face the world. Through love that small place expands and "makes one little room an everywhere." Why stray too far when everything meaningful is right there in front of you? The odes of John Keats, Wallace Stevens, William Carlos Williams, W.H. Auden and Elizabeth Bishop, and of course John Ashbery and James Schuyler, helped shape my sensibility. The elements of celebration and loss, the permanent and the ephemeral, along with a search for an elevated experience embedded in the ordinary — the uncanny in the clear light of day — that's what moved me. Wallace Stevens said it for me in his late poem, "To an Old Philosopher in Rome" where the speaker of the poem stands on a threshold of the street and the threshold of Heaven. After enumerating the objects in the reductive space of this philosopher's humble room — the books, the bed, the table, the candle and the flame tearing at the wick — he praises the doubleness of experience and the sensuality of perception, what Stevens calls "the illumined large in the veritable small."

Particulates 1 + 2, 1997
Oil, alkyd, acrylic, modeling
paste, varnish on cotton
and canvas
2 parts, 11 x 3.5 x 3.5"
and 5 x 3.5 x 3.5"
Collection of Gabriele &
Giuseppina Caccia Dominioni,
Milan

IB Where does your experience surface in
the paintings?

JS At the time that I started making pieces
like the matchbooks I was living in a very
confined, cave-like space in Chelsea. There
were many homeless, disenfranchised and
discarded people all around the streets and
on the subway. Mail would appear under
the door at a certain time of the day. It had
a feeling of living in an absurd theater piece. I was reading novels
by Don Delillo and Paul Auster and could identify with the frag-
mentary, alienated experiences that they were describing. A character that stands out from Paul Auster's novella "City of Glass,"
came in retrospect to be somewhat emblematic for me. This old
man is observed wandering about the city without destination,
picking up seemingly random scraps of paper, wrappers, pieces
of urban detritus with no apparent rhyme or reason; he preserved
what was meant to be overlooked. In the end we realize that his
movements traced an arcane, deliberate pattern. I realized after
the fact that I was something like that "urban archeologist,"
concentrating on disposable things, things not meant to be saved
or closely examined. I was taking anonymous, mass-produced
shards and making them my own. One piece along these lines,
"Withdrawal," is a check from Chemical Bank made out to my
grandmother and myself. Towards the end of her life I was taking
care of her banking and paying her bills. After she died, we thought
we had withdrawn all of the money, and forgot about the account.
Years later, I received this check for a dollar in the mail which I
never cashed. The shower cap, "Andy's Mom," reminds me of her.

IB There is a nineteenth century still-life painting in this exhibition,
An Office Board for Smith Brothers Coal Company, 1879, by John
Peto. What is it about his rack pictures that attracts you?

JS I found the frontality of these American tromp l'oeil paintings

forthright and compelling, imagining how they would hang in
the setting that they were painted in to create a strange doubling.
Except for the frame, there could be a seamless transition between
the depicted and the actual. In Peto's Office Board, for example,
the objects in his painting appear to be actual size. I responded to
the humbleness or banality of the imagery and the modernness of
that heightened attention to detail. It represented society; it was
commonplace, not very high flown. You've got cartes de visites,
music scores, envelopes, tags, ribbons, the residue of parlor room
activities, bits of ephemera that I was attracted to. On the surface
it's very bland, but the ordinariness is poignant to me like experience lost in time.

When I started making "Apology With Scraps," I made up the
headline "I'm So Sorry" but took other elements from the New
York Post, The New York Times, or things found in my wallet or
in the gutter. As I made it I wasn't looking directly at Harnett or
Peto, but I wanted to do something that conjured that gestalt in
my mind with an awareness of paintings by Robert Ryman and
how he analyzed the relationship of the painted plane and the
wall plane. I was interested in making some-
thing that created a relationship between
the wall and the painting using Harnett or
Peto's illusionism as a back-story, fusing these
elements together in this actual "collage."

Zenith, 1993
Powdered graphite, stand
and linseed oil on canvas;
lacquer on aluminum
14 x 11 x 1.75"
Collection of the artist

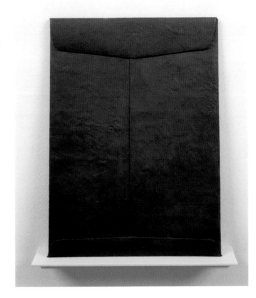

IB Why the phrase "I'm so Sorry?" and how
much of the piece is revealing autobiography;
I see your grandmother's check reappears.
How do these details relate to the found or
"chance" details?

JS Don't we all have something to be sorry
about? It seemed like an absurdly wet utter-
ance for a front page, something that could
provide comic relief for all that potential
heaviness. We are always displaying our

autobiography — it's inescapable. Every act is informed by it. On the other hand I found it amusing to put so much out there and still keep my cards close to my chest (the piece is like a torso to me). It hovers midway between personal revelation and parody. After all, individual pain is always hugely persuasive and undeniably real, but it never validates a work of art or places it above critique. What is the truth in art? If a writer creates a character, and let's say that character even assumes one's own name, like Paul Auster, is that character separate and distinguishable from the writer of that story? I think so. My "Apology" raises a question about authorship without necessarily giving anything away. Because my name is on it we make certain assumptions. The ticket up on the top is my Dad's business card. To the right is a card that has my name embossed on it from NYU's Skin and Cancer Unit, which is where my Mom went for chemotherapy before she died of cancer. I wanted the foxmarks of the aging paper to be something like skin, the skin of a painting and the skin of a human. It seems to suggest autobiography but it doesn't add up. I wanted it to have humor and pathos, "tears and hugs." It's kind of anonymous and embarrassing, revealing and concealing, expressive and parodic.

IB Andy Warhol's Brillo boxes have long been an example in discussions about high and low. How did you come to make your refrigerator box, and were these earlier debates an issue in your work?

JS I was walking down Prince Street and I saw a Sub-Zero box in a dumpster. I was stirred to think about the way you see people using things like a box for makeshift shelter and the disparity between the conspicuous consumer and somebody who is living in a very extreme situation. It is a trophy and an empty shell. In this regard, the double entendre in the phrase "Sub-Zero"

(facing page)
John F. Peto (1854–1907)
Office Board for Smith Brothers Coal Company, 1879
Oil on canvas
28.25 x 24"
Addison Gallery of American Art, Phillips Academy, Andover, Massachusetts
Museum purchase, 1956.13

Apology with Scraps, 1995–96
Oil, alkyd, acrylic and modeling paste on canvas; oil, alkyd and laqcuer on mylar and steel; oil, alkyd and acrylic on wood
26 x 4.5 x 19"
On extended loan to the Tang Teaching Museum and Art Gallery from a Private Collection

could connote these disparities: cold and unfeeling at one end of the social spectrum, second-class citizen or even sub-human at the other. Prepackaged notions of social extremes...or the way kids might use a box like this as an imaginary fort or hideout, an arena for fantasy. To make the Brillo box or the tomato soup carton Warhol utilized the most rudimentary form of representation I can imagine. At this distance in time it's hard to believe viewers ever mistook them for actual consumer products — but then again, I never intend to create something that the spectator will mistake for a found object, it merely has to attain a certain level of credibility in order to function. I have no pretension about it being anything other than an art object, to engage the viewer as an object of observation and contemplation and perhaps say something about being human, the pathos of a made thing in space, in a social space. Warhol's mother was an Eastern European immigrant, probably very religious and clean, kept a nice house, hence the Brillo box. I think she lived with him and probably made a lot of soup for him — very wholesome, very 50's. They make this renegade seem rather soft and nostalgic. I hope "Home" functions on those levels at once — visual, aesthetic, metaphoric, social, as a kind of social mirror. In fact I had never owned my own refrigerator when I began the Sub-Zero box.

Flower Bed, 1999
Oil, alkyd, acrylic, modeling paste, varnish and plexiglas on canvas
4 x 10 x 6"
Collection of Daniel Wiener and Alice Kaltman, New York

IB Many of your works are literal containers. Lately they have been taking the form of shopping bags. Do these overtly consumer objects represent our contemporary situation?

JS I like the way they evoke transported-ness, carrying something from one place to another — a resting point between destinations. In this case what they carry is not fixed or solid, but constantly shifting: they convey meaning. What they hold is not "inside," it's all on the surface. I whole-heartedly agree with Duchamp that the spectator completes the work of art,

that the artwork is merely the device or
pivot. It is a platitude to say consumption
is our religion; these pieces are meant to
be seductive, beautiful — a celebration
and a critique. It's not an either/or situation, life is a lot more complicated than
that. As an artist I am frequently moving
between worlds that are not necessarily
mutually exclusive but that rub against
each other somewhat uneasily. I've been
making bags from museums, high-end
boutiques and more vernacular designs
like grocery bags. As an extension of this
body of work I recently experimented with
blown glass in the form of shopping bags.
I like the literal and metaphoric idea of
transparency in the material in relation to

my Freud bag in particular. I also like the way glass suggests a
window, which brings us full circle to "Ut Pictura Poesis," the title
of an Ashbery poem in the collection *Self Portrait in a Convex
Mirror*... make it like a window. It's been my desire to get away
from the idea of the painting as a window and to have the work
exist in the shared space of the spectator. Within this group
"Born To Shop" takes the model of Johns' "Three Flags" and is pretty
upfront in its status as a commodity, but I hope it's seductiveness
wins the viewer over. Ideally it works not as commentary or gloss
but as a thing in itself and on its own terms. To paraphrase something Frank Stella said in Working Space, if it's not sexy, it's not
art. Stated another way, that's all an artwork can do: stimulate.
As we all know in this media culture, a little bit of sex goes a
long way.

Transparent Exchange, 2000
Blown glass
16.5 x 15.5 x 6"
Courtesy of the artist and
Studio La Città, Verona, Italy

*The preceding is excerpted from a dialogue that took place at
The Tang Teaching Museum and Art Gallery at Skidmore College
on April 10, 2001.*

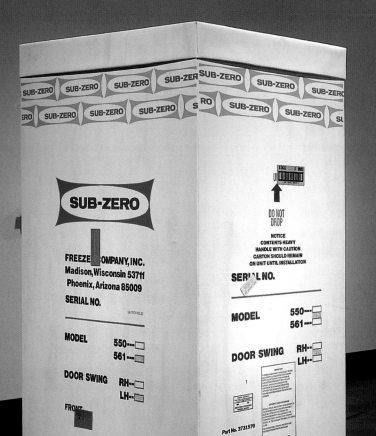

Three Gray Statements, 1994
Powdered graphite, alkyd, stand and
linseed oils on canvas; oil and alkyd
on mylar; lacquer on aluminum
Three parts, each 5.5 x 10.5 x .5"
Collection of the artist

Andy's Mom, 1995–96
(front and back view)
Oil, alkyd, acrylic, modeling paste
and gel medium on canvas;
foam, velvet, wood and steel
20 x 9 x 9"
Collection of the artist

A Ladder of Requests, 1995–96
Oil, alkyd, acrylic, modeling paste
and mylar on canvas over steel
Overall dimensions 112 x 9.5 x 2.25"
The Progressive Corporation,
Cleveland, Ohio

Ut Pictura Poesis?, 2001
Oil, alkyd, acrylic and modeling paste
on canvas mounted on aluminum
3.25 x 6.5"
Courtesy of the artist and
Jack Shainman Gallery, New York

Home, 1996
Oil, alkyd, acrylic and modeling paste
on canvas
86.5 x 30.5 x 40.5"
On extended loan to the Tang
Teaching Museum and Art Gallery
from a Private Collection

Super Citrussy, 1997
Oil, alkyd, acrylic, modeling paste
and varnish on canvas; latex on wood
79 x 5.75 x 5.75"
Collection of the artist

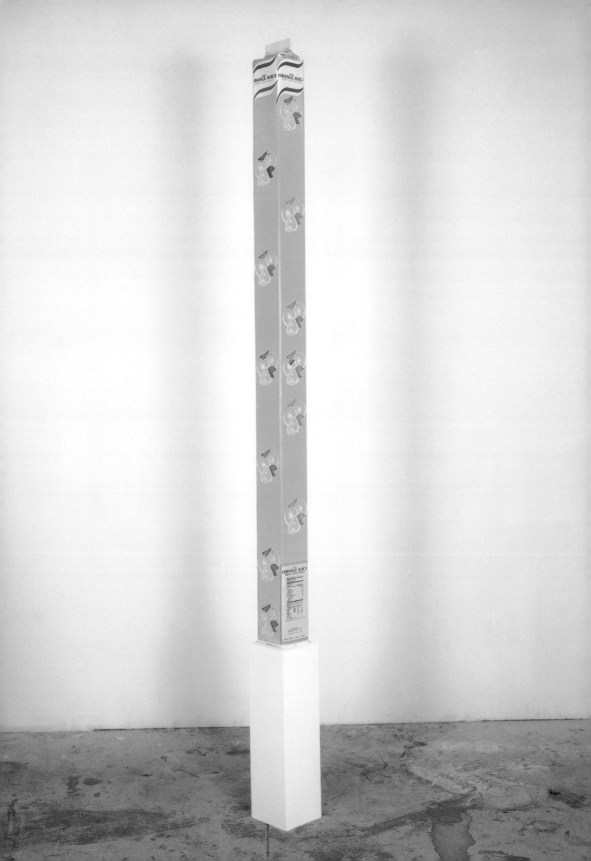

Floor Model, 1997–99
Oil, alkyd, acrylic and modeling paste
on canvas
14 x 12.5 x 9"
Collection of the artist

Berry Basket, 1998
Oil, alkyd, acrylic and modeling paste
on canvas
19 x 10 x 10"
The Panza Collection, Lugano

Bivouac, 1998
Oil, alkyd, acrylic and modeling paste
on canvas; velvet, foam, wood, lacquer
on steel
23.75 x 9.25 x 6"
Collection of Claude Simard

Timberline, 1999
Acrylic and varnish on museum board;
oil, acrylic and modeling paste on wood
4.5 x 101 x 1.25"
The Bailey Collection, Toronto

Bird in Space, 1999
Oil, alkyd, acrylic, modeling paste and
varnish on canvas; latex on wood
84 x 7 x 7"
Collection of Paul and Charlotte Corddry

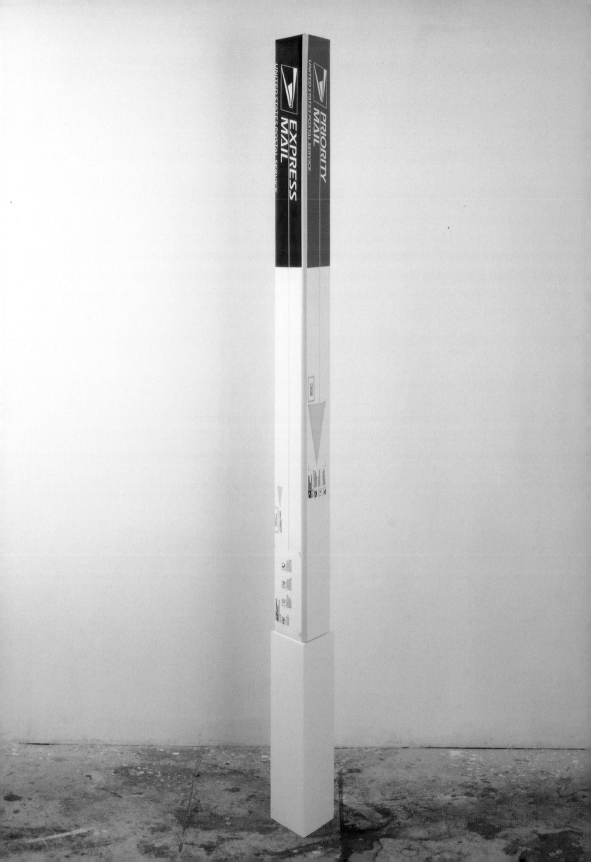

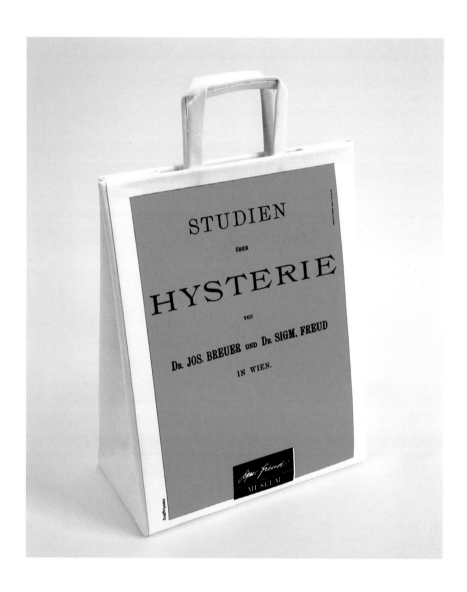

The Ghost in the Machine (after Joseph Kosuth), 2000
(front and back view)
Oil, alkyd, acrylic and modeling paste
on canvas
19 x 12 x 7"
Private Collection, New York

DREI ABHANDLUNGEN ZUR
SEXUALTHEORIE

VON

PROF. DR. SIGM. FREUD

IN WIEN

Posey, 2000
Oil, alkyd, acrylic and modeling paste
on canvas
10.5 x 11.25 x 12"
Collection of Dorothy Bandier, New York

Plea, 1998
Oil, alkyd, acrylic, modeling paste
on canvas
1.5 x 13 x 15"
Private Collection, Stuttgart

Politeness Counts, 2000
Oil, alkyd, acrylic and modeling paste
on canvas
25 x 11 x 4"
Collection of Vera List

Shirley, 2000
Oil, alkyd, acrylic, modeling paste
and varnish on canvas
68 x 29 x 29"
Collection of Vicki and Kent Logan

Snowblind, 2000
Oil, alkyd, acrylic, modeling paste and
wax on canvas; acrylic and polyester resin
19 x 22 x 5"
Private Collection, New York

Born to Shop, 1999
Oil, alkyd, acrylic, modeling paste
and varnish on canvas; lacquer
and wax on bronze
21 x 20.75 x 8"
The Panza Collection, Lugano

Snowman, 2000
Acrylic, modeling paste and varnish
on canvas; lacquer on aluminum
68.5 x 31 x 25"
Collection of Beth Rudin DeWoody

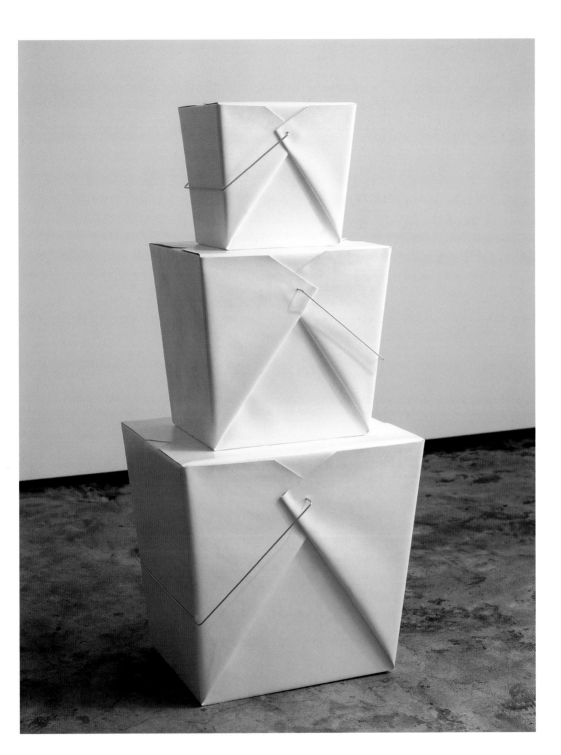

Hello Kitty (Odalisque), 2001
Acrylic and modeling paste
on canvas; lacquer on steel
5 x 101.5 x 8"
Courtesy of the artist and
Jack Shainman Gallery, New York

Note to Self #5, 2001
Oil, alkyd, acrylic, modeling paste
on canvas mounted on aluminum
2.5 x 4.5"
Courtesy of the artist and
Jack Shainman Gallery, New York

Please
Do Not Touch
The Art

Prison Garb (Real Cashmere), 2001
Oil, alkyd, acrylic and modeling
paste on muslin and canvas
15.5 x 16 x 6.25"
Courtesy of the artist and
Angles Gallery, Santa Monica

Woman on a Divan, 2001
Oil, alkyd, acrylic and modeling paste
on muslin and canvas
6.5 x 22 x 13"
Courtesy of the artist and
Angles Gallery, Santa Monica

The Whale (Chris Farley in Heaven), 2001
Oil, alkyd, acrylic and modeling paste
on canvas
39 x 26 x 10"
Courtesy of the artist and
Jack Shainman Gallery, New York

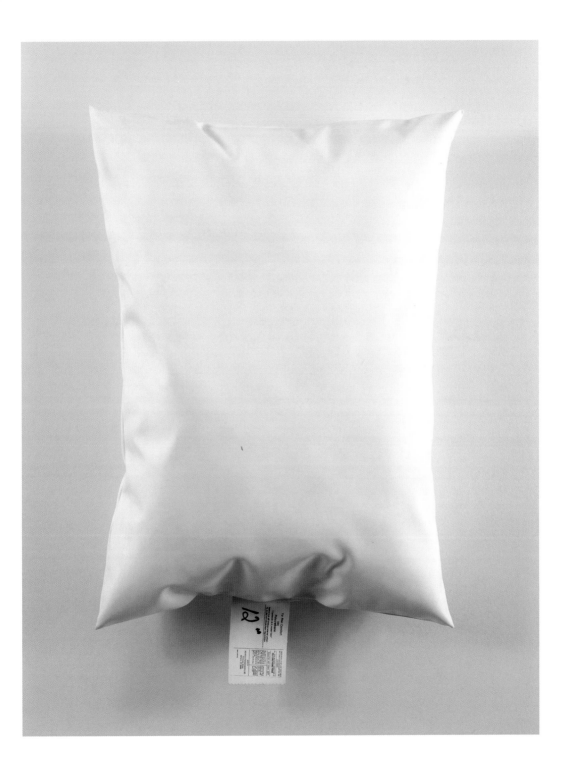

All works by Jonathan Seliger unless otherwise noted. All dimensions in inches H x W x D

1. *Three Gray Statements*, 1994
Powdered graphite, alkyd, stand
and linseed oils on canvas; oil
and alkyd on mylar; lacquer on
aluminum
Three parts, each 5.5 x 10.5 x .5
Collection of the artist

2. *Andy's Mom*, 1995–96
Oil, alkyd, acrylic, modeling paste
and gel medium on canvas; foam,
velvet, wood and steel
20 x 9 x 9
Collection of the artist

3. *A Ladder of Requests*, 1995–96
Oil, alkyd, acrylic, modeling paste
and mylar on canvas over steel
Overall dimensions 112 x 9.5 x 2.25
The Progressive Corporation,
Cleveland, Ohio

4. *Apology with Scraps*, 1995–96
Oil, alkyd, acrylic and modeling
paste on canvas; oil, alkyd and
laqcuer on mylar and steel; oil,
alkyd and acrylic on wood
26 x 4.5 x 19
On extended loan to the Tang
Teaching Museum and Art Gallery
from a Private Collection

5. *Home*, 1996
Oil, alkyd, acrylic and modeling
paste on canvas
86.5 x 30.5 x 40.5
On extended loan to the Tang
Teaching Museum and Art Gallery
from a Private Collection

6. *Super Citrussy*, 1997
Oil, alkyd, acrylic, modeling
paste and varnish on canvas;
latex on wood
79 x 5.75 x 5.75
Collection of the artist

7. *Floor Model*, 1997–99
Oil, alkyd, acrylic and modeling
paste on canvas
14 x 12.5 x 9
Collection of the artist

8. *Little Colossus*, 1997–98
Oil, alkyd, acrylic and soluvar on
polyester resin and fiberglass;
latex on wood
Overall dimensions 12.75 x 18 x 10
Collection of the artist

9. *Bivouac*, 1998
Oil, alkyd, acrylic and modeling
paste on canvas; velvet, foam,
wood, lacquer on steel
23.75 x 9.25 x 6
Collection of Claude Simard

10. *Bird in Space*, 1999
Oil, alkyd, acrylic, modeling
paste and varnish on canvas;
latex on wood
84 x 7 x 7
Collection of Paul and
Charlotte Corddry

11. *Timberline*, 1999
Acrylic and varnish on museum
board; oil, acrylic alkyd and
modeling paste on wood
Overall dimensions 4.5 x 101 x 1.25
The Bailey Collection, Toronto

12. *The Ghost in the Machine
(after Joseph Kosuth)*, 2000
Oil, alkyd, acrylic and modeling
paste on canvas
19 x 12 x 7
Private Collection, New York

13. *Politeness Counts*, 2000
Oil, alkyd, acrylic and modeling
paste on canvas
25 x 11 x 4
Collection of Vera List

14. *Posey*, 2000
Oil, alkyd, acrylic and modeling
paste on canvas
10.5 x 11.25 x 12
Collection of Dorothy Bandier,
New York

15. *Shirley*, 2000
Oil, alkyd, acrylic, modeling paste
and varnish on canvas
68 x 29 x 29
Collection of Vicki and
Kent Logan

16. *Snowblind*, 2000
Oil, alkyd, acrylic, modeling paste
and wax on canvas; acrylic and
polyester resin
19 x 22 x 5
Private Collection, New York

17. *Snowman*, 2000
Acrylic, modeling paste and
varnish on canvas; lacquer
on aluminum
68.5 x 31 x 25
Collection of Beth Rudin
DeWoody

18. *Hello Kitty (Odalisque)*, 2001
Acrylic and modeling paste
on canvas; lacquer on steel
5 x 101.5 x 8
Courtesy of the artist and
Jack Shainman Gallery, New York

19. *The Whale (Chris Farley
in Heaven)*, 2001
Oil, alkyd, acrylic and modeling
paste on canvas
39 x 26 x 10
Courtesy of the artist and
Jack Shainman Gallery, New York

20. *Note to Self #1–6*, 2001
Oil, alkyd, acrylic and modeling
paste on canvas mounted
on aluminum
Various dimensions
Courtesy of the artist and
Jack Shainman Gallery, New York

21. *Ut Pictura Poesis?*, 2001
Oil, alkyd, acrylic and modeling
paste on canvas mounted
on aluminum
3.25 x 6.5
Courtesy of the artist and
Jack Shainman Gallery, New York

22. John F. Peto (1854–1907)
*Office Board for Smith Brothers
Coal Company*, 1879
Oil on canvas
28.25 x 24
Addison Gallery of American
Art, Phillips Academy, Andover,
Massachusetts
Museum purchase, 1956.13

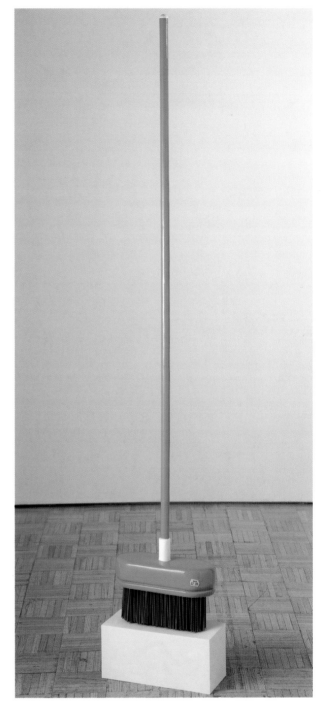

Housekeeping, 1996. Oil, alkyd, acrylic, modeling paste, epoxy resin and soluvar on canvas over
plastic and foam; lacquer on steel; latex on wood, 73.5 x 5.5 x 11.25". Collection of the artist.

JONATHAN SELIGER

Born, New York, New York, 1955
Lives and works in Brooklyn, New York

Education

1978

B.A., State University of New York at Binghamton

Solo Exhibitions

2001

Floor Model, The Tang Teaching Museum and Art Gallery, Skidmore College,
    Saratoga Springs, New York
Personal Shopper, Angles Gallery, Santa Monica, California
Haines Gallery, San Francisco, California

2000

Studio la Città, Verona, Italy
Claudia Gian Ferrari, Milan, Italy
Jack Shainman Gallery, New York, New York

1999

Jack Shainman Gallery, New York, New York

1997

Schmidt Contemporary Art, St. Louis, Missouri

1996

Bravin Post Lee, New York, New York
Anders Tornberg, Lund, Sweden
Studio la Città, Verona, Italy

1995

Thomas Solomon's Garage, Los Angeles, California

1994

Bravin Post Lee Gallery, New York, New York

1993

Craig Cornelius, New York, New York

For A Family, 1995–96
Oil, alkyd, acrylic, modeling
paste, and varnish on canvas;
lacquer on steel
44.5 x 19 x 19"
Collection of the artist

Selected Group Exhibitions

2001

Studio La Città, Verona, Italy

24th International Print Biennial, Ljubljana, Slovenia

2000

New Prints 2000, International Print Center, New York, New York

Simultaneous, Jack Shainman Gallery, New York, New York

Recent Gifts from Eileen & Peter Norton, Weatherspoon Art Gallery,
    University of North Carolina at Greensboro

Tamarind: 40 Years, University of New Mexico Art Museum, Albuquerque,
    New Mexico

*The Perpetual Well: Contemporary Art From the Collection of the Jewish
    Museum*, traveled to: Samuel P. Harn Museum of Art, Gainesville, Florida;
    Sheldon Memorial Art Gallery, University of Nebraska, Lincoln, Nebraska;
    Parrish Art Museum, Southampton, New York; and Huntington Museum
    of Art, Huntington, West Virginia

Post Pop, Susquehanna Art Museum, Harrisburg, Pennsylvania

1999

Zolla/Lieberman Gallery, Chicago, Illinois

The Conversation, Jack Shainman Gallery, New York, New York

Matter of Time, Dorsky Gallery, New York, New York

Live from New York, Haines Gallery, San Francisco, California

The Farm Show, CSPS, Cedar Rapids, Iowa

Showroom, The Arts Center of the Capital Region, Troy, New York

1998

Bravin Post Lee Gallery, New York, New York

Laissez-Faire, Printed Matter, New York, New York

Blooming, Karen McCready Fine Art, New York, New York

The Everyday Sublime, Barbara Krakow Gallery, Boston, Massachusetts

Zolla/Lieberman Gallery, Chicago, Illinois

Food, Marcel Sitcoske Gallery, San Francisco, California

1997

A Private View, Kent Gallery, New York, New York

Word and Image/Word as Image, Jane Vorhees Zimmerli Art Museum,
    Rutgers University, New Brunswick, New Jersey

Normatic, One Great Jones, New York, New York

Stepping Up, Andrew Mummery Gallery, London, England

Onomatopoeia, Studio la Città, Verona, Italy

The Packaged Vernacular, Patricia Faure Gallery, Santa Monica, California

1996

20" x 15", Anna Kustera Gallery,
    New York, New York
Lemberg Gallery, Birmingham,
    Michigan
Subversive Domesticity, Wichita
    Art Museum, Wichita, Kansas
Alice's Looking Glass, Apex Art,
    New York, New York
Selections from the Panza Collection,
    Trento Museum, Trento, Italy

1995

Oddi Bagnoli, Rome, Italy
Still Life-Portrait-Landscape, Bravin Post
    Lee Gallery, New York, New York
Other Choices Other Voices, Islip Art Museum, East Islip, New York
Wheel of Fortune, Lombard Fried Gallery, New York, New York

1994

Serial, Angles Gallery, Santa Monica, California
De-Pop, Cummings Art Center, Connecticut College
Domestic Setting, Los Angeles, California
New from New York, Montgomery Glasoe Fine Art, Minneapolis, Minnesota
Site Seeing, Bardamu Gallery, New York, New York
For Appearance Sake, Horodner-Romley, New York, New York
Reveillon, Stux Gallery, New York, New York

1993

Transient Decor: Room 311, Roger Smith Hotel, New York, New York
Media Message, Wooster Gardens, New York, New York

1992

Writing on the Wall, 303 Gallery, New York, New York
Mssr. B's Curio Shop, Thread Waxing Space, New York, New York
Ecstasy Shop, Dooley Le Capellaine, New York, New York
Invitational '92, Stux Gallery, New York, New York

1991

Ornament, John Post Lee Gallery, New York, New York

Installation view, *Personal
Shopper*, Angles Gallery,
Santa Monica, May 2001

Installation view,
Jack Shainman Gallery,
New York, March 2000

Selected Bibliography

2001

Muritti, Elisabetta, ELLE Italia, April.

Hirsch, Faye, *Art On Paper*, January–February, p. 74.

Meyers, Terry, "Painting Is in The Bag," Studio la Città
    & Claudia Gian Ferrari Arte Contemporanea (exhibition catalogue).

2000

Baker, Kenneth, "Fears, Hopes — Address Unknown," *San Francisco Chronicle*,
    Saturday, January 22, pgs. B1 & B10.

1999

Cotter, Holland, "Matter of Time," *The New York Times*, September 10.

Perchuk, Andrew, *Matter of Time*, Dorsky Gallery, New York, New York
    (exhibition brochure).

1997

Reed, Michael, "The Packaged Vernacular," *Artnews*,
April, p.24.

Belli, Gabriela and Giuseppe Panza, eds., *The Panza di
Biumo Collection: Some Artists of the 80's and 90's*,
Trento Museum, Electa (exhibition catalogue).

1996

Kimmelman, Michael, "Jonathan Seliger at Bravin Post
Lee," *The New York Times*, December 20, p. C28.

Levin, Kim, "Jonathan Seliger at Bravin Post Lee,"
Voice Choices, *The Village Voice*, December 17.

Meneghelli, Luigi, "Tanto Per Un'Idea Dell'Arte Actuale,"
L'Arena, Cultura & Societa, November 6, p. 35.

Self, Dana, *Subversive Domesticity*, The Ulrich Museum
of Art, Wichita State University, Wichita, Kansas
(exhibition catalogue).

Newhall, Edith, "Talent," New York Magazine, December
9, p. 104.

Ostrow, Saul, *Mssr. B's Curio Shop*, Thread Waxing
Space, New York, New York (exhibition catalogue).

Nilsson, Torgny, "Naer duken blir objekt," *Nord Vastra
Skanes Tidningar*, January 23.

Sandberg, Lotte, "Popkunstens etterbilder," *Oslo
Dagbladet*, August 28.

Agrell, Alexander, "Seliger Foervandlar Vardagens
Ting Till Konst," *SYDSVENSKAN*, January 14.

1995

"Jonathan Seliger, Manadens konst," *Noejesguiden*,
December.

Markus, Liz, "Jonathan Seliger," *The New Art Examiner*,
September, p. 47.

1994

Levin, Kim, "Jonathan Seliger," *The Village Voice*, April 18.

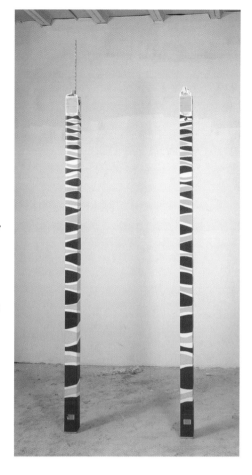

Ma and Pa (American Gothic),
2001
Oil, alkyd, acrylic, modeling paste
and varnish on canvas
2 parts, 112.5 x 3.75 x 3.75 and
99 x 3.75 x 3.75"
Courtesy of the artist and
Jack Shainman Gallery, New York

ACKNOWLEDGEMENTS

Jonathan Seliger: Floor Model is the first in the *Opener* series of exhibitions that brings artists to the Tang Teaching Museum and Art Gallery to work alongside Skidmore College students. As an interdisciplinary museum we provide new possibilities and contexts for the presentation and at times creation of artwork. It is in this spirit that we invited Jonathan Seliger to discuss his influences with the college community which led to the inclusion of an important nineteenth century still life painting within a large group of his work. Jonathan has also completed a new series of paintings for the exhibition that directly engage the practice of museums.

Any museum project is the result of a collaboration between many individuals and this exhibition and catalogue are no exception. We are very fortunate to have the oppurtunity to bring together works that span many years of Jonathan's career. Thank you to Bruce Bailey, Dorothy Bandier, Paul and Charlotte Corddry, Vera List, Vicki and Kent Logan, Joel and Sherry Mallin, Douglas Maxwell, The Progressive Corporation, Beth Rudin DeWoody, Jack Shainman Gallery, Claude Simard, and an anonymous private collector for their generous loans. I would especially like to thank Kate Shepherd for introducing me to Jonathan's work and to Jack Shainman for his consistent support of this project. I would also like to thank Adam Weinberg, Director of the Addison Gallery of American Art for his support of the Tang Teaching Museum and the generous loan of John Peto's *An Office Board for Smith Brother's Coal Company*. Also thank you to the Friends of Tang for their support of the exhibition program.

Bethany Johns has guided and designed an exquisite catalogue with beautiful photographs by Arthur Evans, Jerry Stuart, John Bessler, Jeff Sturges, and John Berens. Every member of the Tang staff has helped with this exhibition, special thanks to Barbara Rhoades, Gayle King, Susi Kerr, Chris Kobuskie, Brian Caverly, Gavin McKeirnan, and Jennifer O'Shea. Also thanks to student interns, Daniel Byers, Cindy Fifield, Michael Flanagan, Joshua LeFrancois, Ariel Magnes, and Lauren Restrepo. Thank you to Barbara Melville in college relations and Barry Pritzker and Paul Hanks in Advancement for their support. Special thanks to Charles Stainback, Director of the Tang for his encouragement and trust and lastly to Jonathan Seliger for his enthusiasm, and wonderful artwork that continues to inspire and illuminate. The project is the result of a true collaboration.— IAN BERRY, *Curator*

I am indebted to many people: Nancy Seliger and Jerry Finkelstein, Stan and Edith Seliger, John and Rochelle DiRe, Kate Shepherd and Miles McManus, Bill Adams, Kerry Schuss, Craig Cornelius, Hélène de Franchis and the staff at Studio La Città, Claudia Gian Ferrari and the staff at Gian Ferrari Arte Contemporanea, Cheryl Haines and the staff at Haines Gallery, David McAuliffe and the staff at Angles Gallery, Dr. and Mrs. Giuseppe Panza di Biumo, Giuseppina and Gabriele Caccia Dominioni, Will Mentor, Ron Yakir, David Humphrey, Daniel Wiener, Fabian Marcaccio, John Post Lee and Karin Bravin. Thanks also to Charles Stainback and the superb staff at the Tang Museum, and each of the lenders who helped make this exhibition possible. Special thanks to Jack Shainman, Claude Simard, Tim Clifford, Judy Sagal and Katie Glicksburg at Jack Shainman Gallery for their ongoing support and facilitation of so many details pertaining to this exhibition. Lastly, none of this would have been concieivable without Ian Berry. Thank you for your vision, patience, generous spirit, intelligence and warm sense of collaboration. I am extremely grateful.

— JONATHAN SELIGER

This catalogue accompanies the exhibition

JONATHAN SELIGER: *FLOOR MODEL*
June 16 – August 26, 2001

The Tang Teaching Museum and Art Gallery
Skidmore College
815 North Broadway
Saratoga Springs, New York 12866

©2001 The Tang Teaching Museum and Art Gallery
ISBN 0-9708790-4-0

Front cover:
Apology with Scraps, 1995–96
Oil, alkyd, acrylic and modeling paste on canvas; oil, alkyd and
laqcuer on mylar and steel; oil, alkyd and acrylic on wood
26 x 4.5 x 19"
On extended loan to the Tang Teaching Museum and Art Gallery
from a Private Collection

Back cover:
Sweet Dreams, 2000
Oil, alkyd, acrylic and modeling paste on canvas
7 x 19 x 27.5"
The Bailey Collection, Toronto

Photographs by Jerry Stuart, John Besler, Jeff Sturges, and John Berens.
Pages 1 and 63, black and white photographs by Jonathan Seliger and
John Bessler, 1994. Pages 14 and 15, installation view, The Tang Teaching
Museum and Art Gallery, Skidmore College, by Arthur Evans.

Designed by Bethany Johns
Printed in Germany by Cantz